Forever Your.
BAR HARBOR

Historic Postcard Images of Mount Desert Island & Acadia

by Earl Brechlin

ISLANDPORT PRESS

Copyright © 2016 Earl Brechlin
2021 printing
ISBN: 978-1-952143-12-0
Library of Congress Control Number: 2016933406
All images courtesy of Earl Brechlin unless otherwise noted.
Printed in the USA.

Islandport Press
P.O. Box 10
Yarmouth, Maine 04096
www.islandportpress.com
info@islandportpress.com

Dean Lunt, Publisher
Teresa Lagrange, Book designer

*To my brother Carl who sparked my
interest in all things old and cool.*

FOREWORD

MORE THAN A CENTURY AGO, years before people began carrying early Kodak Brownie cameras, postcards were a favorite way to document trips and adventures. People collected, as well as, sent postcards to share with others the wonders and sights they had seen. The brightly colored cards, some even tinted by hand, allowed vacationers to relive their trips and bring their friends and families along, again and again.

The popularity of postcards exploded with numerous merchants and photographers competing to offer the widest selection and best views. Initially, many of the cards were produced in Germany. Later, printers in the United States joined the craze. Most of the postcards shown in this book come from the peak postcard period, between 1905 and 1920.

Because of its popularity as a watering hole for the rich and famous, Bar Harbor in its Golden Age was one of the most photographed locations in Maine. Everything from the steamships, to the hotels, to the natural wonders of the island that would later become home to Acadia National Park, was photographed and turned into a postcard which could be mailed for a penny. Today these postcards are recognized not just for their historical content, but also as works of art in and of themselves.

For people today, collecting antique postcards from Bar Harbor, or from anywhere for that matter, is a comparatively inexpensive way to hold onto a piece of the past. The affection they engender creates a bond to the past in much the same way the beauty and history of these special places continue to hold onto our hearts. The images in this book, while never intended as a comprehensive scholarly collection, provide a wonderful taste, a visual sampling if you will, of the way things were in Bar Harbor and on Mount Desert Island more than one hundred years ago.

—Earl Brechlin

HISTORY OF MOUNT DESERT ISLAND

BY ALL ACCOUNTS, MAINE'S WABANAKI TRIBE was the first to visit Mount Desert Island. Evidence of their seasonal encampments, primarily shell heaps, have been found across the area. French explorer Samuel de Champlain first passed through the area in September 1604, giving the island its name *Isle de Monts Deserts,* literally "island of barren mountains." In 1613, a French Jesuit mission attempted to establish a colony near Southwest Harbor but the group was attacked by the English. Other notable French entrepreneurs, including Antoine de la Mothe Cadillac, who went on to found Detroit, also staked a claim to MDI.

The first permanent settlement was established in Somesville in 1761. Bar Harbor, and indeed all of Mount Desert Island, was first put on the map in the mid 1800s by a group that became known as the "Rusticators." Hudson River School artists such as Thomas Cole, Fitz Henry Lane and Frederic Church boarded with area farmers as they produced the sketches and studies needed to create masterpieces that would inspire legions of people to come see the spectacular beauty for themselves. Before long, farmhouses became inns and enterprising businesspeople began building successively larger establishments. This hotelier boom culminated with Bar Harbor's Rodick House that boasted 500 rooms.

Smaller, more private accommodations on hotel properties were often called cottages. Aided by the ease of travel by railroad and steamboat, soon the rich and famous decided to put down deeper roots spurring an upsurge of building as the owners of each grand summer "cottage" sought to one-up the others in terms of size, space, and opulence.

That era, roughly from 1860 until approximately 1925, was known as Bar Harbor's Golden Age. It also coincided with the rise of the Penny Postcard as a way to connect with the folks back home and preserve images from what for many visitors, was the trip of a lifetime.

Bar Harbor, Maine. Birdseye View from Strawberry Hill.

EDEN

THE VILLAGE OF BAR HARBOR, which until 1918 was officially named Eden, as seen from Strawberry Hill looking north over the athletic fields toward Bar Island. Eden was founded on February 23, 1796 when the northern half of the island split off from the town of Mount Desert. The first permanent settlement was established on Mount Desert Island in 1761 at what is now Somesville.

Harbor View showing U. S. War Vessels.

Greetings from Bar Harbor, Me.

BAR HARBOR
MAINE

GREAT WHITE FLEET

U.S. Navy torpedo boats and destroyers lay at anchor in Frenchman Bay off Bar Harbor. The Great White Fleet, a popular nickname for the Navy during the early 1900s, was a frequent visitor to island waters. Today, more than 140 ocean liners carrying 250,000 passengers and crew members drop anchor off Bar Harbor each year.

Arrival of Boat at Bar Harbor, Me.

BAR HARBOR
MAINE

HANCOCK POINT

THE ARRIVAL of a Maine Central Railroad steamer, which sailed from the rail terminus at Hancock Point located across the bay, was always a big event. The names of the wealthy and powerful who landed at the wharf, located at what is today's town pier, were published regularly in the local paper.

Bar Harbor, ME.
Docks at Bar Harbor.

LOCAL PIERS

PRIVATE WHARVES AND PIERS clogged Bar Harbor as shown in this view looking west from the site of the present-day municipal pier. Passenger steamers, private yachts and even canoes were everywhere. Today, excursion and whale-watching boats share the space with private yachts, lobster boats, and kayaks.

M. C. R. R. Wharf, Bar Harbor, Me.

AGAMONT PARK

THIS VIEW OF THE MAINE CENTRAL RAILROAD wharf, taken from the foot of what is now Agamont Park, shows an early souvenir stand as part of the terminal facilities. Today, commercial sales are banned on the town pier that now occupies the spot.

Mt. Desert Bridge, Maine, One of the few toll bridges now in existence

TOLL BRIDGE

GETTING ONTO MOUNT DESERT ISLAND by road was not for the faint of heart near the turn of the 20th Century. This original wooden toll bridge (10 cents for a horse and rider), built in 1837, was taken over by Hancock County in 1917. An estimated 8,000 people attended the dedication and the unveiling of a plaque that stated, "This bridge is dedicated to the soldiers, sailors and marines of Hancock County." The plaque was incorporated into the current bridge when it was built in 1957. The deck and railings on the bridge were extensively rebuilt in 1996.

Bar Harbor, Me.

BAR ISLAND

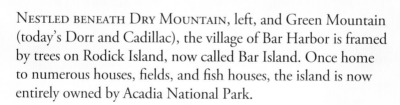

NESTLED BENEATH DRY MOUNTAIN, left, and Green Mountain (today's Dorr and Cadillac), the village of Bar Harbor is framed by trees on Rodick Island, now called Bar Island. Once home to numerous houses, fields, and fish houses, the island is now entirely owned by Acadia National Park.

The Swimming Tank and St. Sauveur Hotel, Bar Harbor, Me;

SWIMMING CLUB

Bar Harbor's swanky swimming club, with its shore-side salt water pool, as seen from Bar Island. The gravel bar to the island is exposed and walkable only at low tide. The large hotel visible in the center is the St. Sauveur, located on Mount Desert Street. The hotel was built in 1870 and torn down in 1945. The road at the far right is Bridge Street.

Courtesy of the Bar Harbor Historical Society.

Bar Harbor, Maine. The Bar and Town from Rodicks Island.

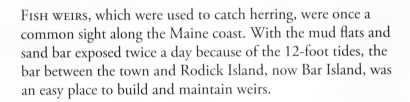

FISH WEIRS

FISH WEIRS, which were used to catch herring, were once a common sight along the Maine coast. With the mud flats and sand bar exposed twice a day because of the 12-foot tides, the bar between the town and Rodick Island, now Bar Island, was an easy place to build and maintain weirs.

Bar Harbor Bar, Bar Harbor, Me.

ISLAND "COTTAGES"

THREE OF THE TOWN'S stately summer homes grace the shore where Bridge Street meets the bar. Despite the large size of these structures, some boasting more than two dozen rooms, elaborate landscaping, and servants' quarters, they were referred to as "cottages" by their wealthy owners. The first private cottages were erected in 1865, with a period of intense construction starting in 1880. The so-called "Cottage Era," lasted through World War I until fading with onset of the Great Depression and, later, World War II. The town once boasted more than 100 summer palaces.

BAR HARBOR, Me. Main Street from Village Green.

THE VILLAGE GREEN

BAR HARBOR'S VILLAGE GREEN, seen on the left, still sports the E. Howard and Company clock donated by the Village Improvement Society. The view is looking north down Main Street from the corner of Mount Desert Street. The Grand Central Hotel once occupied the land that is now the park. The wooden hotel, built in 1873, was torn down in 1906 and the area it occupied was given over as public space.

from Clara i ome not deed

BAR HARBOR
MAINE

HOSE WAGON

THE BAR HARBOR FIRE DEPARTMENT was formed in 1881.
Horse-drawn equipment included a steam engine pumper and
a separate wagon to carry hose. In the 1880s, the department's
competitive hose team, the Orioles, won numerous awards.
Early firefighting focused on saving surrounding structures.
On October 8, 1881 crews fought flames that leveled the
125-room Rodick House Hotel in just an hour. Some firefighters
got tangled in a barbed-wire fence "causing a good many
well-disposed men to use bad language," according to a
newspaper account.

Engine House, Bar Harbor, Me.

FIRE STATION

BAR HARBOR'S FIRE STATION on Firefly Lane, near the Village Green, was designed by architect Fred Savage. Built in 1912, it was home to steam-powered fire engines and teams of horses. The top of the tower was removed in 1951. Today, it sports an addition on the east (right) side that houses the police department and public restrooms.

COURTESY OF THE BAR HARBOR HISTORICAL SOCIETY.

MAIN STREET

MAIN STREET WAS A BUSY PLACE in the early part of the 20th Century. The town's population peaked in 1910 at 4,441 and gradually declined to 3,716 by 1970. At the turn of the next century it boomed again, reaching 5,235 in 2010. The original First National Bank Building with its white columns (center), was hailed as the town's first "fireproof" building.

High School Building, Bar Harbor, Me.

NEW HIGH SCHOOL

THE THREE-STORY BRICK HIGH SCHOOL, which
now serves as the town's municipal building, was dedicated in
1908. This new high school on Cottage Street replaced a two-
story wood structure on High Street, which was later converted
to a Masonic Hall. Bar Harbor High School, designed by noted
local architect Fred Savage, was described in one architectural
journal "as one of the handsomest and most modern school-
houses in Maine." Its educational use ended in 1968 when
students from all over Mount Desert Island began attending
a new, regional high school.

CONGREGATIONAL CHURCH, MT. DESERT ST., BAR HARBOR, ME.

FIRST AUTOMOBILES

TRAFFIC IS HEAVY ON MOUNT DESERT STREET in front of the Bar Harbor Congregational Church just a few years after a bitter political fight ended with automobiles finally being allowed onto Mount Desert Island. The summer community kept "infernal combustion" engines off MDI by supporting a state law prohibiting horseless carriages from using all but one road. Another law prohibited cars from being moved across wharfs or boat ramps. The state legislature changed the law in 1913.

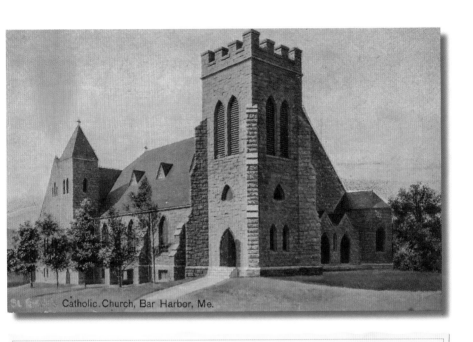

Catholic Church, Bar Harbor, Me.

CATHOLIC CHURCH

LOCATED AT THE CORNER of Ledgelawn Avenue and Mount Desert Street in Bar Harbor, Holy Redeemer Church was built on the site of St. Sylvia's Catholic Church (established in 1881). St. Sylvia's was torn down and the cornerstone of the current granite church was laid by Bishop Louis Walsh on August 11, 1907. The Gothic Revival structure was designed by Victor Hodgins of Bangor. It could seat 800 worshipers. The nearby St. Edwards Convent was added in 1916 and is now the home of the Bar Harbor Historical Society Museum.

St. Mary's by-the-Sea, Northeast Harbor, Maine.

NORTHEAST HARBOR
MAINE

ST. MARY'S BY THE SEA

St. Mary's By the Sea, located on South Shore Road in
Northeast Harbor was consecrated Aug. 24, 1902. The chapel,
now on the National Register of Historic Places, was designed
by Maine architect Harry Vaughn and incorporated granite
removed from a nearby road project. Worship is only held in
the structure during warmer months. The Episcopal parish also
includes St. Jude's Church in nearby Seal Harbor. A related
chapel, named St. James in the Woods, in the long-lost village
of Sound, was built in 1903. Located on Route 198, it was sold
and became a private home in 1987.

Bar Harbor, Maine. The Casino and Bridge Street.

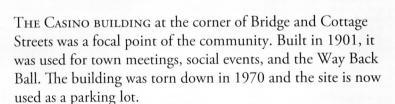

CASINO BUILDING

THE CASINO BUILDING at the corner of Bridge and Cottage Streets was a focal point of the community. Built in 1901, it was used for town meetings, social events, and the Way Back Ball. The building was torn down in 1970 and the site is now used as a parking lot.

Art Building, Bar Harbor, Me.

BUILDING OF THE ARTS

BAR HARBOR'S SPECTACULAR BUILDING OF THE ARTS was designed by Guy Lowell and built in 1907. Located on the south end of Hamilton Hill, adjacent to Kebo Valley Golf Course, the wooden building burned in the Great Fire of 1947. A flat, open site, now private property, is all that remains.

Bar Island, Bar Harbor, Me.

PADDLING

CANOES STORED UPSIDE DOWN on a dock provide visual evidence of a favorite Bar Harbor pastime at the turn of the 20th Century. In 1900, the town's famous Canoe Club boasted more than 300 members and paddling lessons were sometimes taught by area Wabanaki. Homes can be seen on Rodick Island, now Bar Island, in the background.

Newport House and Shaw Path, Bar Harbor, Me.

SHORE PATH

THE TOWN BEACH and beginnings of the Shore Path, seen in the foreground, look much the same today. What has changed are the buildings. The Newport House, left, was built in 1869 and torn down in 1938. There is a parking lot there today. The tall tower at right, is on the Rockaway Hotel, built in 1870. The Rockaway, located on the east side of what is now Agamont Park, was torn down in 1916.

Steel Pier
Bar Harbor M.E.

BAR HARBOR
MAINE

THE READING ROOM

TODAY, A MODERN WHARF in front of the Bar Harbor Inn sits close to the site of this steel pier, which was built in the late 1880s and torn down in 1930. President William Howard Taft came ashore at the steel pier during his visit in 1910. A private club on the grounds, The Reading Room, was actually a front so summer cottagers would have a place to socialize and drink alcohol during Prohibition.

BALANCE ROCK

BALANCE ROCK can still be found along the Shore Path at the foot of Grant's Park, also known as Albert's Meadow. This granite boulder is a very different type of rock than the sedimentary strata it rests upon. Geologists believe it is a glacier erratic, meaning that it was deposited here by a retreating glacier.

Hardy's Point, Bar Harbor, Me.

TOW PATH

HARDY'S POINT ALONG THE SHORE PATH is located on the property of the Bar Harbor Inn. The Shore Path, also called the Tow Path in early manuscripts and cards, begins at the municipal pier and stretches for three quarters of a mile to Wayman Lane. The path is maintained by the Village Improvement Society and is open to the public through the graciousness of private landowners along the route.

Bar Harbor, Me. Shore Path, Bar Island in Distance.

REEF POINT

THE REEF POINT ESTATE WAS BUILT on this property along the Shore Path in Bar Harbor in 1883 for Mary Cadwalader Jones, and was eventually owned by her daughter, the renown landscape architect Beatrix Farrand. The estate was eventually torn down. As seen in the background, an adjacent estate owned by Thomas Musgrave, featured a stone and wood tower. The tower, built in 1881, was also later torn down.

Malvern Hotel
Bar Harbor M.E.

THE MALVERN HOTEL

THE MALVERN HOTEL ON KEBO STREET, south of Mount
Desert Street, was built in 1882. It boasted numerous
"cottages," of up to 14 rooms each. It burned in the Great
Fire of 1947. A senior citizens' housing complex is located
there now.

BAR HARBOR, ME.   BELMONT HOTEL.

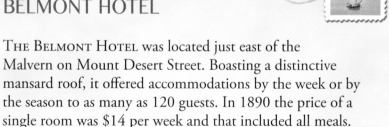

BELMONT HOTEL

THE BELMONT HOTEL was located just east of the
Malvern on Mount Desert Street. Boasting a distinctive
mansard roof, it offered accommodations by the week or by
the season to as many as 120 guests. In 1890 the price of a
single room was $14 per week and that included all meals.
A salon for the entire season could be had for $75. The Belmont
was destroyed in the Great Fire of 1947.

Thank you for the collar it is very pretty. Happy New

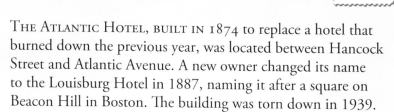

BAR HARBOR
MAINE

ATLANTIC HOTEL

THE ATLANTIC HOTEL, BUILT IN 1874 to replace a hotel that burned down the previous year, was located between Hancock Street and Atlantic Avenue. A new owner changed its name to the Louisburg Hotel in 1887, naming it after a square on Beacon Hill in Boston. The building was torn down in 1939.

Bar Harbor, Maine. The De Gregoire.

DE GREGOIRE HOTEL

THE DE GREGOIRE HOTEL WAS NAMED AFTER THE WOMAN who once held title to half of Mount Desert Island—Marie Therese De Gregoire, daughter of French explorer Antoine de la Monthe Cadillac. The De Gregoire Hotel was located on the northeast side of the intersection of Eden and West Streets. The hotel opened in 1907 and was destroyed in the Great Fire of 1947. The area is trees and field now.

BAR HARBOR, ME. HOTEL FLORENCE AND VILLAGE GREEN.

HOTEL FLORENCE

THE HOTEL FLORENCE, LOCATED ON MAIN STREET directly across from the Village Green, was built in 1887. The rambling wooden structure burned in 1918 except for a portion of the building seen at the far left. Retail shops line the area now.

Greetings from Bar Harbor.

THE INDIAN VILLAGE.

WABANAKI

Mount Desert Island's original summer visitors were members of Wabanaki tribes who thronged to seasonal encampments along the shore. As land values increased in the late 1800s, the Wabanaki found themselves pushed away from the ocean to less desirable areas. This image was taken near the present site of the Bar Harbor Athletic Fields off Main Street after the Wabanaki moved their encampment from the shore near the Bar Island sand bar.

Blaireyrie, Bar Harbor, Me. Residence of D. C. Blair.

BLAIREYRIE

LAVISH SEASON "COTTAGES," sprang up on every shore and hilltop in Bar Harbor during the resort town's golden age. Blaireyrie was built in 1888 near present day Highbrook Road. Purchased by New York banker De Witt Clinton Blair in 1901, it was demolished in 1935 as income taxes and the waning attentions of a new generation of wealthy cottagers prompted the area to lose favor. A large, modern hotel occupies the site now.

Ban-y-Bryn, Bar Harbor, Me.

BAN-Y-BRYN

AMONG THE MANY INDUSTRIALISTS who made their fortunes in railroads and summered in Bar Harbor was Albert Clifford Barney of Cincinnati and Washington, D.C. He commissioned the imposing, granite-walled Ban-y-Bryn on Norman Road in 1888. His wife Alice, a darling in arts circles, soon eclipsed him on the social scene. The "cottage," sported 27 rooms including seven bedrooms and five bathrooms. It also boasted five fireplaces, a stable, and rooms for seven servants. The house, filled with antiques, was among the 68 stately homes destroyed in the Great Fire of 1947.

"Devilstone," Bar Harbor, Me.

DEVILSTONE

LOCATED ON THE TOWN'S storied Shore Path, Devilstone was built for May Bowler, wife of the late George Pendleton Bowler of Cincinnati, in 1885. Henry Vanderbilt leased the home for a summer escape not long after it was built. Reportedly worried about Bar Harbor being too rustic, Vanderbilt brought along a chef and waiters from New York's famous Delmonico's Restaurant to prepare meals. In 1968, the original section of the house was torn down and the library turned into a small cottage. It remains a private home.

Mossley Hall, Bar Harbor, Me.

MOSSLEY HALL

BUILT ON A HILL on Norman Road in 1882, with a sweeping view of the town and bay beyond, Mossley Hall was owned by civil engineer William B. Howard of Chicago. His firm built the Indiana State House and, according to newspaper accounts, "he laid more miles of railroad track than any man in the country." The house, described by noted architecture critic Vincent Scully as "a 19th-century romantic landscape painter's ideal of an upland dwelling," was designed by William Ralph Emerson. It was torn down in 1945.

"The Tides", Bar Harbor, Me.

THE TIDES

THE BAR HARBOR TIDES, now a bed & breakfast, was
built in 1887 and was considered a classic example of Greek
Revival architecture. It overlooks the Bar Island sand bar on
West Street, an area that was known in the late 1800s as
"Millionaires Row." Built for shoe manufacturer merchant
William B. Rice of Boston, the home was a Rotch & Tilden
design. After his death, Rice's wife Gertrude remodeled the
house to reflect a Colonial Revival style.

BRIAR CLIFFE, BAR HARBOR, MAINE.
RESIDENCE OF EDWARD MC LEAN.

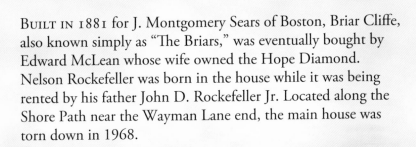

BRIAR CLIFFE

BUILT IN 1881 for J. Montgomery Sears of Boston, Briar Cliffe, also known simply as "The Briars," was eventually bought by Edward McLean whose wife owned the Hope Diamond. Nelson Rockefeller was born in the house while it was being rented by his father John D. Rockefeller Jr. Located along the Shore Path near the Wayman Lane end, the main house was torn down in 1968.

Stanwood, Home of late James G. Blaine, Bar Harbor, Me. '09

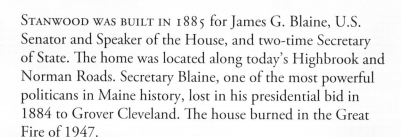

STANWOOD

STANWOOD WAS BUILT IN 1885 for James G. Blaine, U.S. Senator and Speaker of the House, and two-time Secretary of State. The home was located along today's Highbrook and Norman Roads. Secretary Blaine, one of the most powerful politicans in Maine history, lost in his presidential bid in 1884 to Grover Cleveland. The house burned in the Great Fire of 1947.

The Turrets, Bar Harbor, Me.

TURRETS

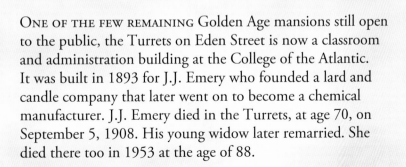

ONE OF THE FEW REMAINING Golden Age mansions still open to the public, the Turrets on Eden Street is now a classroom and administration building at the College of the Atlantic. It was built in 1893 for J.J. Emery who founded a lard and candle company that later went on to become a chemical manufacturer. J.J. Emery died in the Turrets, at age 70, on September 5, 1908. His young widow later remarried. She died there too in 1953 at the age of 88.

Fabbri Cottage, Eden Street, Bar Harbor, Me.

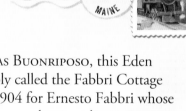

FABBRI COTTAGE

ALTHOUGH ITS FORMAL NAME WAS BUONRIPOSO, this Eden
Street waterfront home was simply called the Fabbri Cottage
by townspeople. It was built in 1904 for Ernesto Fabbri whose
brother Alessandro established a transatlantic radio station at
Otter Cliffs. A monument still notes his accomplishment at a
picnic area in Acadia National Park. The house, which suffered
major damage in a fire in 1918, was rebuilt. It was torn down
in 1963.

JOSEPH PULITZER

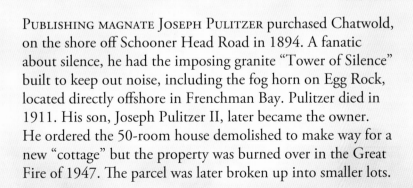

PUBLISHING MAGNATE JOSEPH PULITZER purchased Chatwold, on the shore off Schooner Head Road in 1894. A fanatic about silence, he had the imposing granite "Tower of Silence" built to keep out noise, including the fog horn on Egg Rock, located directly offshore in Frenchman Bay. Pulitzer died in 1911. His son, Joseph Pulitzer II, later became the owner. He ordered the 50-room house demolished to make way for a new "cottage" but the property was burned over in the Great Fire of 1947. The parcel was later broken up into smaller lots.

KENARDEN

KENARDEN, CREATED FROM THE NAME KENNEDY and garden, was built in 1892 for the then-princely sum of $200,000. It featured its own electric power plant. Owner John Stewart Kennedy of New York made his millions in banking and rail-roads. At one time he was the largest stockholder of both the Northern Pacific and Great Northern railroads. The home was later sold to Dr. John Thompson Dorrance who invented condensed soup for Campbell's.

ITALIAN GARDEN, BAR HARBOR, MAINE

54176

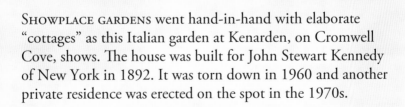

ITALIAN GARDEN

SHOWPLACE GARDENS went hand-in-hand with elaborate "cottages" as this Italian garden at Kenarden, on Cromwell Cove, shows. The house was built for John Stewart Kennedy of New York in 1892. It was torn down in 1960 and another private residence was erected on the spot in the 1970s.

Garden at Beau Desert, Bar Harbor, Me.

BAR HARBOR
MAINE

BEAU DESERT

THE ORNATE GARDEN at Beau Desert, an estate on the shore along Eden Street, looks to be the perfect place for children to play. The house and grounds were built in 1882 for Walter Gurnee. The house was torn down in 1938. The site later became an Oblate Seminary. Vestiges of the gardens are still visible in the property's latest incarnation—College of the Atlantic.

KEBO VALLEY CLUB

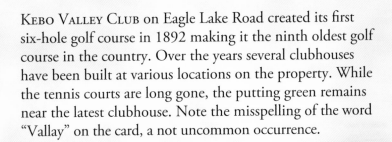

KEBO VALLEY CLUB on Eagle Lake Road created its first six-hole golf course in 1892 making it the ninth oldest golf course in the country. Over the years several clubhouses have been built at various locations on the property. While the tennis courts are long gone, the putting green remains near the latest clubhouse. Note the misspelling of the word "Vallay" on the card, a not uncommon occurrence.

Golfing at Bar Harbor, Me.

PRESIDENT TAFT

PRESIDENT WILLIAM HOWARD TAFT, sporting a bow tie in the center, played Kebo Valley during his visit in July of 1910. He is shown on the 16th green with the Building of the Arts in the background. President Taft set a new "record" right after this photo was taken, shooting a 27 on the par four 17th.

arrived home
all night
be glad.

Swimming Pool
Bar Harbor M E

BAR HARBOR SWIM CLUB

BUILT IN 1903, the tony Bar Harbor Swim Club on West Street boasted a saltwater pool where water was let in at high tide and then kept so it could warm up. Tennis games were also popular. The club was eventually replaced by the Bar Harbor Club. That building remains along West Street, just east of Bridge Street.

ATHLETIC FIELDS

BAR HARBOR'S TOWN ATHLETIC FIELDS were given to the
community by the owners of Kenarden (See page 44). The
image was taken from along Park Street near the site of the
present day Mount Desert Island YMCA. The house on
Strawberry Hill in the distance was likely the spot where the
view of town on page 1 was taken.

Bar Harbor Horse Show.

HORSE SHOW

THE BAR HARBOR HORSE SHOW was the peak event of the
summer season. It was held over three days each August
in Morrell Park, named for Col. Edmund Morrell of
Philadelphia. A viewing box with less than a dozen chairs
costs the princely sum of $500. The grounds and racetrack
were located at the foot of Champlain Mountain where the
renowned Jackson Laboratory is now located.

The Ovens, Mt. Desert Island, near Bar Harbor, Me.

SALISBURY COVE
MAINE

THE OVENS

THE WABANAKI CALLED this rock formation the "Devil's Oven" and believed it was an entrance to hell. Located at the base of cliffs between Hulls and Salisbury Coves, these wave-sculpted cuts and a small natural bridge were popular destinations for cottagers' afternoon jaunts. They are only accessible at low tide, and are located on private property not open to the public.

Sand Beach and Bee Hive Mountain, Bar Harbor, Me.

SAND BEACH

SAND BEACH IN ACADIA NATIONAL PARK was privately owned until after the Great Fire of 1947. It is now one of the most popular natural attractions in a park that sees as many as 2.7 million visitors a year. In 1911, the schooner *Tay*, with a cargo of lumber and shingles, wrecked on the beach with the loss of one life. The ribs of the schooner can still be seen jutting from the dunes after fierce winter storms.

The Ocean Drive.

Bar Harbor, Me.

ACADIA MAINE

PARK LOOP ROAD

WHEN FIRST CREATED, this portion of the Ocean Drive on the Acadia National Park Loop Road was open to two-way traffic. The park, which was the vision of summer residents George B. Dorr and Charles Eliot, came to be in no small measure thanks to the financial support of John D. Rockefeller Jr. His crews built many sections of motor roads as well as the carriage road system.

LAFAYETTE NATIONAL PARK.　　　　Copyright A. S. Dockham—Plate B.

AMERICAN EAGLES IN NEST, MT. DESERT ISLAND, ME.

ACADIA NATIONAL PARK

ACADIA NATIONAL PARK started out in 1916 as Sieur de Monts
National Monument. It became Lafayette National Park in
1919. The name was changed to Acadia in 1929. The park has
long been home to endangered species such as the American
Bald Eagles, shown above. Endangered Peregrine falcons are
now nurtured and protected by the park.

Bicycle Path, Bar Harbor, Me.

Handcolored

BICYCLE PATH

ACADIA MAINE

THE WOODS AND HILLS of Acadia National Park are filled with the remnants of long-lost trails and paths. Among them is a once popular bicycle path that skirted the Bear Brook Beaver Dam Pond, at the north end of Champlain Mountain. Built in 1895 under the direction of one of the park's founders, George B. Dorr, the path passed the original location of the Wild Gardens of Acadia. The gardens, which feature labeled examples of the area's native trees, shrubs, and other vegetation were later moved to Sieur de Monts Spring. The bicycle path area was devastated by the Great Fire of 1947.

DUCK BROOK BRIDGE

THE DUCK BROOK BRIDGE is a spectacular, three-arch structure some 200 feet in length. Built in 1929 at a cost of $77,800, the bridge features a 40-foot wide central arch flanked by smaller spans. The pink granite façade includes parapets where visitors can look down at the rushing stream below. Considered to be the most refined of the 16 unique spans on Acadia National Park's carriage roads, the bridge provides access to the Witch Hole Pond loop that is popular with bikers, walkers, and cross-country skiers.

THUNDER HOLE CAVE, OCEAN DRIVE, BAR HARBOR, MAINE   123346

THUNDER HOLE CAVE

THUNDER HOLE ALONG THE OCEAN DRIVE in Acadia National Park is one of most-visited locations in the park. Incoming waves funnel down a narrow cleft and ram into a shallow cave at the end. The surging water compresses air in the cave that can produce a ground-shaking "whooomp" and a geyser of spray shooting back out sometimes as high as 40 feet into the air. Heavy swells and an incoming tide produce the best display.

The Mountain Road, Acadia National Park   Mt. Desert Island, Me.

LOWER MOUNTAIN ROAD

Now called the Lower Mountain Road, this section of the Acadia National Park Loop Road between Cadillac Mountain and Jordan Pond was one of the first stretches completed in 1924. Eagle Lake is to the right with Pemetic Mountain on the left. From the start, planners wanted the park to be accessible by automobile. Initially only a gravel way, it was eventually paved and now stretches for total of 22 miles.

Bee Hive Mt., Mt. Desert Island, On the "Ocean Drive" near Bar Harbor, Me.

BEEHIVE

THIS OLD FARMSTEAD near Great Head and Sand Beach was already crumbling when this photo was taken around 1910. The mountain in the back is the Beehive. At the time, it sported more tree cover than today due to changes caused by the Great Fire of 1947. A later structure near the site is now used by the park service to house seasonal rangers.

BEACHCROFT PATH, BAR HARBOR, MAINE.   82564

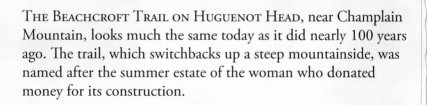

ACADIA
MAINE

BEACHCROFT TRAIL

THE BEACHCROFT TRAIL ON HUGUENOT HEAD, near Champlain Mountain, looks much the same today as it did nearly 100 years ago. The trail, which switchbacks up a steep mountainside, was named after the summer estate of the woman who donated money for its construction.

Mt. Desert Island, Maine; The Bubbles.

THE BUBBLES

THE BUBBLES, seen from the lawn of the Jordan Pond House, form one of the most distinctive ridge lines in New England. A farmhouse built on the site in 1896 became known as The Jordan Pond House and was famous for tea and popovers. Its walls, lined with birch bark, sowed the seeds of its own destruction when the building burned in 1979. A new, larger facility with a restaurant, tea lawn, and gift shop now occupies the site.

STEPPING STONES ACROSS OUTLET TO SIEUR-DE-MONTS TARN, BAR HARBOR, MAINE. 82552

ACADIA
MAINE

DORR MOUNTAIN

SEVERAL TRAILS up Dorr Mountain, formerly called Dry Mountain and Flying Squadron Mountain, can be accessed after crossing these stepping stones at the outlet of the Tarn near Sieur de Monts Spring in Acadia National Park. Park co-founder George Dorr created a small dam at the stepping stones to help create a reflecting lake out of a swampy area.

6817 A LILY POND   BAR HARBOR, MAINE.

CANOEING

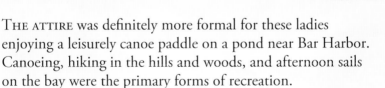

THE ATTIRE was definitely more formal for these ladies
enjoying a leisurely canoe paddle on a pond near Bar Harbor.
Canoeing, hiking in the hills and woods, and afternoon sails
on the bay were the primary forms of recreation.

COURTESY OF THE BAR HARBOR HISTORICAL SOCIETY.

9070
The Village Park,
Bar Harbor, Me.

EARLY VILLAGE GREEN

BAR HARBOR's wonderful Village Green was created in 1906 after a massive hotel was torn down. In the background can be seen the town's first fire station, erected in 1882. The E. Howard and Company clock with its wood casing remains in place today. The clock was installed for the centennial celebration of the town, then called Eden, in 1896. The town band plays free concerts here on Thursday evenings during summer.

JORDAN POND HOUSE

WITH VERANDAS offering a sweeping vista of Jordan Pond and the Bubbles, the lawn at the Jordan Pond House has been hosting tea, with its famous popovers, since it was opened by the McIntire family around 1895. The former farmhouse sported a rustic atmosphere with the bark of white birch trees for wallpaper. The national park service acquired it in 1940. When a fire leveled it in 1979, the current restaurant and gift shop was rebuilt with the help of private donations.

OTTER CREEK GORGE FROM HUGUENOT HEAD, BAR HARBOR, ME.

HUGUENOT HEAD

GOING FOR "TRAMPS"—long hikes with friends with an emphasis on good conversation—was a popular activity during Bar Harbor's heyday. Here a group pauses near the top of Huguenot Head on the Beachcroft Trail to admire the view to the south towards Otter Creek.

COURTESY OF THE BAR HARBOR HISTORICAL SOCIETY.

BAR HARBOR, ME.   SCHOONER HEAD.

BRIGHAM COTTAGE

Schooner Head off Schooner Head Road sported far fewer trees than today in this view showing the Brigham Cottage. The cottage burned in the Great Fire of 1947. The high headland to the right is now occupied by a large private seasonal residence.

SUMMIT ROAD

LEGEND HOLDS that so much dynamite was used for one blast to make this cut on the Cadillac Mountain Summit Road in Acadia National Park that it cracked stone foundations miles away in Bar Harbor. Various methods have been used to get up the mountain including a cog railway and a toll road for horse-drawn carriages. Cadillac is the highest point on the North Atlantic Seaboard.

MOUNTAIN ROAD

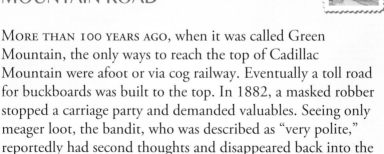

MORE THAN 100 YEARS AGO, when it was called Green Mountain, the only ways to reach the top of Cadillac Mountain were afoot or via cog railway. Eventually a toll road for buckboards was built to the top. In 1882, a masked robber stopped a carriage party and demanded valuables. Seeing only meager loot, the bandit, who was described as "very polite," reportedly had second thoughts and disappeared back into the woods. Despite a $5,000 reward, he was never caught.

Sieur de Monts Spring, Acadia National Park   Mount Desert Island, Maine

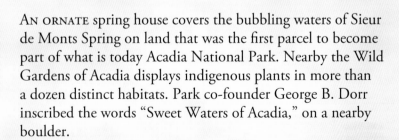

SIEUR DE MONTS

AN ORNATE spring house covers the bubbling waters of Sieur
de Monts Spring on land that was the first parcel to become
part of what is today Acadia National Park. Nearby the Wild
Gardens of Acadia displays indigenous plants in more than
a dozen distinct habitats. Park co-founder George B. Dorr
inscribed the words "Sweet Waters of Acadia," on a nearby
boulder.

ALONG THE BLUFFS, BAY DRIVE, BAR HARBOR, MAINE

117171

BLUFFS ROAD EDEN STREET

ORIGINALLY EYED as a route for a trolley line that was never built, a road across "The Bluffs" in Bar Harbor affords a spectacular view of upper Frenchman Bay. Now designated State Route 3, it is the primary access road to Bar Harbor. It was once called Corniche Drive. Across the Bay, in Hancock, a Nazi submarine landed two spies in 1941 on a mission to steal atomic bomb secrets. They were quickly spotted and arrested in New York City by the FBI.

Visit Summit Tavern at Summit of Cadillac Mountain.
Here one can secure an Official Booklet of Acadia National Park.
Souvenirs, Photographs and Post Cards are on sale.
Sodas and Light Lunches served.

SUMMIT TAVERN, SUMMIT OF CADILLAC MOUNTAIN, ACADIA NATIONAL PARK, BAR HARBOR, ME.

SUMMIT TAVERN

THE SUMMIT TAVERN was the last of a series of privately owned and operated structures to grace the top of Cadillac Mountain in Acadia National Park. Over the years buildings have included multi-story wooden hotels. In 1940 the entire top of the mountain was taken over by the U.S. Army for a top secret radar station to watch for Nazi submarines. The only buildings at the summit now are a small gift shop, restroom, and a radio transmitter shack.

Bar Harbor, Maine. Eagle Lake from Currens Cove.

EAGLE LAKE

ROWBOAT RENTALS on Eagle Lake were all the rage.
The device at left in a cove at the Northwest corner of the lake,
is part of a conveyor owned by a company that harvested ice
from the lake until the 1950s. Part of the sluiceway remains
on the bottom and can be seen when the light is right and the
water is low. The lake today is a public water supply that bans
swimming and wading.

Egg Rock Light, Bar Harbor, Me.

EGG ROCK LIGHT

BUILT IN 1875, Egg Rock Lighthouse consists of a 40-foot brick tower surrounded by a wood-frame keeper's house. Built on a 12-acre treeless ledge in the middle of Frenchman Bay, its flashing red beacon welcomes the more than 140 cruise ships that make port calls each season. The original foghorn was powered by steam. In 1887, a gale swept over the island, carrying away the outhouse, henhouse and other small structures. Storms regularly move rocks estimated to weigh more than 30 tons. The light was automated in 1976.

Old Gun, at Schooner Head, Bar Harbor, Me.

OLD GUN

BAR HARBOR'S WEALTHY SUMMER RESIDENTS
worried about attack at the outbreak of the Spanish American
War in 1898. Several Civil War-era cannons, including this
15,000-pound Rodman at the Hale Estate on Schooner Head,
were positioned to guard Frenchman Bay. Another was placed
on Turtle Island near Winter Harbor and two on Egg Rock.
The war ended before fortifications were complete. The gun
was scrapped in 1943. The two on Egg Rock were removed
by helicopter in 1991 and now guard the seaward approach to
Agamont Park in town.

Anemone Cave, Bar Harbor, Maine

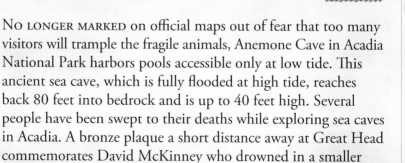

ACADIA
MAINE

ANEMONE CAVE

NO LONGER MARKED on official maps out of fear that too many
visitors will trample the fragile animals, Anemone Cave in Acadia
National Park harbors pools accessible only at low tide. This
ancient sea cave, which is fully flooded at high tide, reaches
back 80 feet into bedrock and is up to 40 feet high. Several
people have been swept to their deaths while exploring sea caves
in Acadia. A bronze plaque a short distance away at Great Head
commemorates David McKinney who drowned in a smaller
cave there in 1969.

North East Harbor, Me., Harbor Drive.

NORTHEAST HARBOR

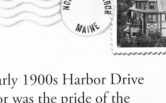

WHEN IT WAS COMPLETED in the early 1900s Harbor Drive on the east side of Northeast Harbor was the pride of the village and made for a much easier trip to Seal Harbor. It is now part of Route 3. Northeast Harbor reportedly got its name because it was located on a cove, "North East," of the town of Southwest Harbor. Over the years people have combined the two directions in each name into one word either "Southwest," or "Northeast."

Cottage Street, Northeast Harbor, Me.

SHINGLE-STYLE COTTAGES

With both sides lined by distinctive shingle-style cottages it is no surprise how Cottage Street in the village of Northeast Harbor got its name. The street is now called South Shore Drive. The houses on the left were privately owned. Those on the right were part of the Kimball House hotel complex. The tower and flag in the distance on the right side of the street is at the Rock End hotel. Both hotels are long gone now.

NORTHEAST HARBOR, ME.   NEIGHBORHOOD HOUSE.

NEIGHBORHOOD HOUSE

THE NEIGHBORHOOD HOUSE shines here shortly after it was built in 1906 in Northeast Harbor. Now a popular community center and provider of children's programs, the Neighborhood House looks much the same today.

Rock End House, No. East Harbor, Me.

ROCK END

THE ROCK END was one of Northeast Harbor's finest hotels when it was completed in 1884. It was originally called the Revere House. The shingle-style hotel featured 83 guest rooms and 27 baths. Located on a ledge overlooking the water at the end of Rock End Road, it burned down in 1942.

KIMBALL HOUSE

LOCATED AT THE CORNER of Kimball Road and South Shore Drive, across from St. Mary's Church, the Kimball House was built in 1886. Boasting 70 guest rooms, it was designed by John Clark of Bar Harbor. The grand old hotel faded from popularity and was torn down in 1966.

North East Harbor, Maine. Sargents Drive, looking up Somes Sound.

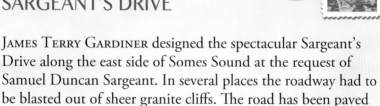

SARGEANT'S DRIVE

JAMES TERRY GARDINER designed the spectacular Sargeant's Drive along the east side of Somes Sound at the request of Samuel Duncan Sargeant. In several places the roadway had to be blasted out of sheer granite cliffs. The road has been paved and widened slightly over the years, so the exact rock formation shown is no longer identifiable.

Mt. Desert, Me. The Old Mill.

THE OLD SAWMILL

LOCAL HISTORIANS are not exactly sure of the location of this old sawmill, which was already falling down when the photo was taken around 1905. Mount Desert Island was home to dozens of mills which produced lumber, wool, flour, and other commodities. The best educated guess is the building was a sawmill built by Ed Somes in Somesville on the stream between Long Pond and Somes Pond. A pond there is called, appropriately enough, Ed's Pond.

848 Somesville, Me.
Main St.

SOMESVILLE

ALONG WITH BEING inarguably the prettiest village in Maine, Somesville bears the distinction of being the first settlement on Mount Desert Island. Abraham Somes built a log cabin in the area where the village now sits in 1761. Except for pavement instead of dirt, and the addition of a few more houses, the village looks much the same today as it did 100 years ago.

FROM THE COLLECTION OF BARBARA SAUNDERS.

SOMESVILLE

WITH NARY A TREE IN SIGHT, the layout of the village of Somesville is easy to see in this view taken from the east side of the harbor. The steeple belongs to the Somesville Union Meeting House which was erected in 1852. The church is still going strong today.

STAR CREVICE, BAR HARBOR, ME.

SALISBURY COVE MAINE

STAR CREVICE

LOCATED IN SALISBURY COVE ON STAR POINT, on the grounds of the Mount Desert Island Biological Laboratory, Star Crevice is a natural opening in the ocean side bedrock. The lab, founded in 1898, relocated to its present location in 1921. In 2013, the non-profit institution was designated a Center for Biomedical Research Excellence. Using marine life models, its scientists are at the forefront of research into tissue repair and regeneration, kidney and heart disease, cancer, and Alzheimer's and Parkinson's disease.

MT. DESERT ISLAND, ME. SOMES' SOUND

SOMES SOUND

SOMES SOUND
MAINE

CONSIDERED THE ONLY TRUE FJORD on the east coast of the
United States, Somes Sound was carved by glaciers that covered
the island with nearly a mile of ice. The deep ocean inlet, which
is several hundred feet deep in places, nearly cuts the island
in two. This view is taken from the north end, looking south.
Brown's Mountain, now called Norumbega, rises on the left,
Robinson Mountain, now called Acadia, rises on the right.

Seal Harbor, Maine. Long Pond west from Road.

LITTLE LONG POND
SEAL HARBOR

MANY FOLKS believe Little Long Pond and the surrounding forest are part of Acadia National Park, but they are protected by a nonprofit called the Land and Garden Preserve of Mount Desert Island. David Rockefeller Sr. donated more than 1,000 acres around the pond to the preserve in 2015 on the occasion of his 100th birthday. The area is open to the public although bicycles are banned to preserve carriage roads.

OTTER CREEK SHOWING CADILLAC AND FLYING SQUADRON MTS., BAR HARBOR, MAINE. LAFAYETTE NATIONAL PARK.

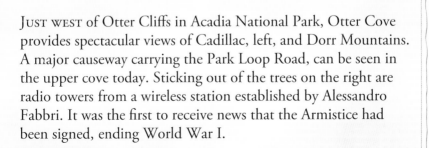

OTTER CREEK AND RADIO TOWERS

JUST WEST of Otter Cliffs in Acadia National Park, Otter Cove provides spectacular views of Cadillac, left, and Dorr Mountains. A major causeway carrying the Park Loop Road, can be seen in the upper cove today. Sticking out of the trees on the right are radio towers from a wireless station established by Alessandro Fabbri. It was the first to receive news that the Armistice had been signed, ending World War I.

Seal Harbor, Me. from Ox Hill.

SEAL HARBOR

BUILDINGS CLUSTER AROUND THE SHORE in Seal Harbor where
only fields and park land remain today. Seal Harbor was first
settled in June of 1809. It was formerly called Clement's
Harbor. The large hotel at the upper right is the Seaside Inn.
The properties were purchased by a Rockefeller family holding
company in 1963 and subsequently torn down.

Sea Side Inn, Seal Harbor, Me.

SEASIDE INN

BUILT IN 1869 and expanded several times, the 100-room Seaside Inn stood slightly up the hill overlooking the Seal Harbor Beach. It was acquired by the Rockefeller family and torn down in 1960s. There is now a field in its former location.

Seal Harbor, Maine. The Library.

SEAL HARBOR LIBRARY

BUILT IN THE SPRING OF 1899, the Seal Harbor Library was constructed on a lot donated by village philanthropists George Cooksey and Sara Clement. The building and furnishings cost $1,595. In the beginning the library was lit with oil lamps. The announcement of the library declared it would be a "good library, free to all, and clear of debt." It was open only in summers at the onset. The inaugural librarian Eva Clement was paid a salary of $1 per week. The first library president was George Stebbins.

Seal Harbor, Maine. The Arch Bridge and Sea Cliff Drive.

RAVEN'S NEST

THIS STUNNING STONE ARCH over a cleft known as Raven's Nest, is the centerpiece of Sea Cliff Drive in Seal Harbor. The road, now owned by the town, was built in 1895 by George B. Cooksey, an English grain dealer from New York, to open up several hundred acres of property he purchased for development. The area is now home to summer cottages owned by the rich and famous.

SEAL HARBOR, ME.   CONGREGATIONAL CHURCH.

CONGREGATIONAL CHURCH

BUILT IN 1902, THE SEAL HARBOR CONGREGATIONAL CHURCH
was designed by Grosvenor Atterbury and built by Charles
Candage. The chapel remained in use until it was sold to a
private buyer in 1989. The congregation still meets in the Abby
Chapel in Seal Harbor.

THE EYRIE

THE EYRIE, THE SPECTACULAR SUMMER HOME of Acadia National Park's main benefactor John D. Rockefeller Jr., started out as a much more modest home. Mr. Rockefeller bought the property, overlooking Little Long Pond in Seal Harbor, in 1910 and immediately began expanding it. Fifty years later, after his death, other family members offered to no avail to give the 100-room house away to any worthy organization or educational institution. It was torn down in 1963.

"Skylands" Summer Home of Mr. Edsel Ford   Seal Harbor, Maine

SKYLANDS

ARCHITECT DUNCAN CANDLER designed this palatial summer
home atop Ox Hill in Seal Harbor for Edsel Ford in 1925.
After changing hands several times, Skylands was most recently
purchased by lifestyle maven Martha Stewart.

Long Pond, Mt. Desert Island, Maine.

LITTLE LONG POND

LITTLE LONG POND IN SEAL HARBOR was created by a natural sea wall of cobble stones thrown up by winter surf. Owned by the Rockefeller family, the fields, forests, and carriage roads around it are open to the public. Mountains reflected in its waters include, from left to right, Jordan Mountain, now called Penobscot, the Bubbles, center, and, right, Black Mountain, now called Pemetic.

COURTESY OF THE BAR HARBOR HISTORICAL SOCIETY.

Main St., S. W. Harbor, Me.

SOUTHWEST HARBOR

SOUTHWEST HARBOR'S MAIN STREET looks much different now than in this circa 1905 view looking north from approximately the corner of today's Wesley Avenue. Much of the downtown changed when a fire in 1922 destroyed five major buildings and damaged others. Southwest Harbor became its own town when it split from Tremont in 1905.

Kronprinzessin Cecilia and U. S. Torpedo Boat Terry, Bar Harbor, Me.

CECILIE

LATER DUBBED BY ROMANCE WRITERS as "The Magic Ship," the German liner [*Kronprinzessin*] *Cecilie* suddenly appeared in Frenchman Bay off Bar Harbor on the morning of August 4, 1914. She fled to the U.S. after her captain learned of the outbreak of WWI. Along with 1,200 passengers, the *Cecilie* carried nearly $14 million in gold and silver. Passengers eventually returned to Boston by train. The ship remained off Bar Harbor until November and later became the troop ship USS *Mount Vernon*.

12. MT. DESERT FROM SUTTON'S ISLAND, MT. DESERT ISLAND, MAINE. 95260

MT. DESERT FROM SUTTON'S ISLAND

SUTTON'S ISLAND IS ONE OF FIVE ISLANDS that make up the town of Cranberry Isles. Two, Islesford and Great Cranberry, are among only 14 islands in Maine that are inhabited year-round. Two other islands off Mount Desert Island, Swan's Island and Long Island, also known as Frenchboro, host permanent communities as well. All are reached by regular ferry service. The Cranberry Isles was given its name by Governor Francis Bernard in 1762 due to a 200-acre marsh full of the native New England fruit. Sutton's was named for Ebenezer Sutton who purchased it in 1755.

Lower Hadlock Pond,
Northeast Harbor, Maine.

LOWER HADLOCK POND

NESTLED HIGH AMONG THE MOUNTAINS above the village, Upper and Lower Hadlock Ponds were the ideal source of fresh water for the Northeast Harbor Water Company when it was formed in 1883. Gravity provided all the power that was necessary to supply "full and ample," pressure to the houses and businesses below. The Mulford Ice Company also used the ponds to harvest giant blocks of ice each winter. For many years in the late-1800s blocks were sent down to ice houses on the edge of the harbor via a half-mile long sluiceway. Today the surrounding area is protected by Acadia National Park.

VALLEY COVE

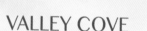

LOCATED ON THE WESTERN SIDE of Somes Sound, Valley Cove has a unique tie to the area's past. Man of War Brook plunges 35 feet into the ocean over cliffs there and was reportedly used by British and French naval vessels to replenish their supply of fresh water. A part of Acadia National Park, it can be accessed by a hiking trail or the gated Man of War Fire Road. Deep and dark woods along the road appear in a scene in the Stephen King movie "Pet Sematary."

Claremont House, S. W. Harbor, Me.

SOUTHWEST HARBOR
MAINE

CLAREMONT HOUSE HOTEL

THE STATELY CLAREMONT HOUSE HOTEL continues to cater to summer visitors from its Clark Point site overlooking Somes Sound. Built in 1884, the building has expanded over the years, including the addition of a restaurant kitchen and dining room. Other houses on the grounds have been converted to guest space. The interior of the hotel underwent a major renovation in 1994. For years, the hotel hosted the weeklong Claremont Croquet Classic each August.

LAROCHELLE

BUILT IN 1909 as a 41-room "cottage" for the Bowdoin family, LaRochelle on West Street is one of the few surviving mansions from Bar Harbor's Golden Age. Purchased by the Bar Harbor Historical Society in 2019, it now offers two floors of exhibits and displays on the history of Bar Harbor, Acadia National Park, and Mount Desert Island. It is the only intact private mansion open to the public.

Underwood & Richardson's Wharfs, McKinley, Me.

UNDERWOOD CANNING WHARF, MCKINLEY

BASS HARBOR in Tremont has always been known as a true, Downeast "working" harbor. One of the busiest facilities was the Underwood Canning plant, here shown when the town was called McKinley. Established in 1889, the plant was soon canning lobster, clams, sardines, and other seafood. After a long abandonment, the brick main building was converted to condominiums.

South West Harbor, Maine. View from foot of High Street, showing Somes Sound.

HIGH ROAD

HIGH STREET, NOW HIGH ROAD, atop a hill on the north side
of the harbor in Southwest Harbor, provides excellent views
to the east across Somes Sound toward Manchester Point in
Northeast Harbor. This portion of the road, and the stone
wall, are now located on private ways not open to the public.

Birdseye view of Manset, Me.

MANSET

MARITIME COMMERCE has always been the hallmark of the village of Manset in Southwest Harbor. Located on the south shore of the harbor, the area today has a high concentration of piers and boating facilities. Boat building leader The Hinckley Company is centered on the shores of the cove in the middle of the view.

544 Southwest Harbor, Me. Ocean House.

OCEAN HOUSE HOTEL

THE OCEAN HOUSE HOTEL was a popular summer place to stay in Manset on the south shore of Southwest Harbor. The hotel, which was built in around 1850, was torn down in the 1940s. It was located at the top of Ocean House Hill Road near the present Catholic Church.

Southwest Harbor, Me. Somes Sound.

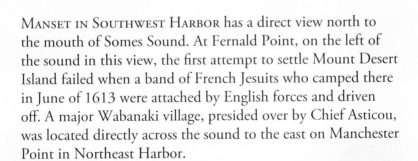

SOMES SOUND

MANSET IN SOUTHWEST HARBOR has a direct view north to
the mouth of Somes Sound. At Fernald Point, on the left of
the sound in this view, the first attempt to settle Mount Desert
Island failed when a band of French Jesuits who camped there
in June of 1613 were attached by English forces and driven
off. A major Wabanaki village, presided over by Chief Asticou,
was located directly across the sound to the east on Manchester
Point in Northeast Harbor.

Mt. Desert, Me. Bass Harbor Head Light.

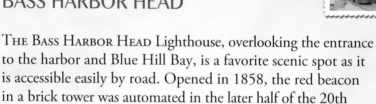

BASS HARBOR HEAD

THE BASS HARBOR HEAD Lighthouse, overlooking the entrance to the harbor and Blue Hill Bay, is a favorite scenic spot as it is accessible easily by road. Opened in 1858, the red beacon in a brick tower was automated in the later half of the 20th century. The grounds are open to the public although the keeper's house is a private residence.

McKinley, Maine. Looking down Bass Harbor.

TREMONT

Tremont, on Mount Desert Island's west side, split off from Mount Desert in 1848. When asked what to name a new post office for the village on the east side of Bass Harbor someone remarked to a federal official "name it after the president [William McKinley] for all we care." Officials did, and the name McKinley stuck until the mid 1960's when residents petitioned Congress and got it changed to Bass Harbor. This view is from the north end of the harbor looking south.

McKinley, Maine. Bernard from McKinley.

BERNARD

THE TREMONT VILLAGE OF BERNARD can been seen across the harbor from Bass Harbor. When Tremont formed in 1848 folks wanted to call it Mount Mansell, after the early English name for all of Mount Desert Island, but that was rejected. The view is from near the site of the existing Maine State Ferry Service Terminal. The ferry runs regularly to Swan's Island and Frenchboro.

McKinley, Maine. Bass Harbor Bay and Western Mt.

THREE PEAKS

TREMONT EVENTUALLY GOT ITS NAME from the three major peaks visible from the harbor including, from left, Bernard Peak, Mansell Peak on Western Mountain, and Beech Mountain. The very first government meeting on Mount Desert Island, then a plantation, was held on Crocket Point in Tremont on March 30 of 1776.

THE BAR HARBOR EXPRESS

AT THE TURN OF THE CENTURY there were two options for travelling to Bar Harbor—train or steamship. The Bar Harbor Express made regular runs to Mount Desert Ferry, a wharf complex at Hancock Point where passengers boarded steamships to get to harbors all around Frenchman Bay including Bar Harbor. The last trains ran in the 1930s and the tracks were torn up long ago.

UNITED STATES COALING STATION, BAR HARBOR, ME.

LAMOINE STATE PARK

CONSIDERED THE FINEST NAVAL coaling facility in the world
when it was finished in 1903, the site of these long docks and
towers are now Lamoine State Park just across the bay from
Mount Desert Island. The facility was capable of holding
60,000 tons of coal for the Great White Fleet. It was demolished
in the 1920s.

"Sappho" at Bar Harbor, Maine.

SAPPHO

STEAMSHIPS SERVING ALL THE TOWNS on Mount Desert Island were the technological stars of their day. Built at Bath Iron Works in 1886, the *Sappho* was one of the most popular—and one of the most infamous. While people were boarding her in August of 1889 at Mount Desert Ferry, the dock gave way, plunging scores of people into the water. Twenty people died.

Bar Harbor, Me., Steamer Norumbega.

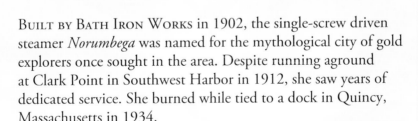

NORUMBEGA

BUILT BY BATH IRON WORKS in 1902, the single-screw driven steamer *Norumbega* was named for the mythological city of gold explorers once sought in the area. Despite running aground at Clark Point in Southwest Harbor in 1912, she saw years of dedicated service. She burned while tied to a dock in Quincy, Massachusetts in 1934.

NORUMBEGA AGROUND

DELAYED BY FOG on August 12, 1912, the Maine Central Railroad steamship *Norumbega* lost power after leaving Northeast Harbor. The *Norumbega* drifted onto a ledge off Clark Point in Southwest Harbor. By low tide, the vessel was high and dry. Captain Joseph Norton, his crew, and the two passengers on board were not hurt. Eventually salvage crews used the wake of the steamer *Moosehead* to rock the *Norumbega* free at high tide.

IROQUOIS AGROUND

The Eastern Steamship Company liner *Iroquois* ran its bow onto the beach of Bald Porcupine Island off Bar Harbor in the fog on the morning of July 13, 1936. She was pulled free on a later high tide. The *Iroquois* went on to become the hospital ship U.S.S. *Solace* and was in Pearl Harbor on December 7, 1941. She later saw service at Iwo Jima. After the war she was repurposed as the liner *Ankara* in Turkey where she was dubbed the "Rose of the Mediterranean." She was scrapped in 1981.

Bar Harbor, Me., Steamer Sieur De Monts.

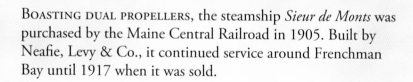

SIEUR DE MONTS

BOASTING DUAL PROPELLERS, the steamship *Sieur de Monts* was purchased by the Maine Central Railroad in 1905. Built by Neafie, Levy & Co., it continued service around Frenchman Bay until 1917 when it was sold.

SUNBEAM

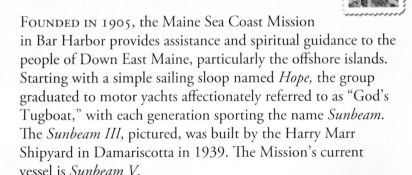

FOUNDED IN 1905, the Maine Sea Coast Mission in Bar Harbor provides assistance and spiritual guidance to the people of Down East Maine, particularly the offshore islands. Starting with a simple sailing sloop named *Hope,* the group graduated to motor yachts affectionately referred to as "God's Tugboat," with each generation sporting the name *Sunbeam.* The *Sunbeam III*, pictured, was built by the Harry Marr Shipyard in Damariscotta in 1939. The Mission's current vessel is *Sunbeam V.*

VIEW OF BAR HARBOR FIRE, OCT. 23, 1947

THE GREAT FIRE OF 1947

THE GREAT FIRE OF 1947 was a seminal moment in Mount Desert Island's history. The fire began in a dump off the Crooked Road in Bar Harbor on October 17. Smoke billows high into the sky from the Crooked Road area in this view from the Bar Harbor Airport in Trenton, on the mainland. The mountains of Acadia National Park are in the background.

VIEW OF BAR HARBOR FIRE, OCT. 23, 1947

MALVERN HOTEL AREA, BAR HARBOR, ME.

WIND WHIPPED DESTRUCTION

CREWS BATTLED the Great Fire for nearly a week but lost about 3,000 acres. Then, on October 23, flames whipped by gale-force winds blackened another 14,000 acres in only eight hours. The Malvern Hotel (see page 27) was destroyed by the fast-moving fire.

VIEW OF BAR HARBOR FIRE, OCT. 23, 1947

DEGREGOIRE HOTEL AREA, BAR HARBOR, ME.

RUINS OF THE DEGREGOIRE

ISLAND FIRE CREWS WERE supported by Army troops, but still could not save most of Bar Harbor from destruction, save for the immediate downtown. With flames and burning trees blocking all roads, some 400 people were evacuated by the sea from the Town Pier. The ruins of the stately DeGregoire Hotel (see page 30) mark the eastern edge of the fire's advance into the Business District.

VIEW OF BAR HARBOR FIRE, OCT. 23, 1947

BELMONT HOTEL AREA, BAR HARBOR, ME.

ROLLING BALL OF FLAME

PARTS OF UTILITY POLES rest in blackened trees near the ruins of the Belmont Hotel (see page 28) after the 1947 fire hit Bar Harbor. Three people died before the firestorm finally ran out of fuel in a rolling ball of flame that pitched over Great Head in Acadia National Park.

FOREST STREET, BAR HARBOR, ME.

17,188 ACRES DESTROYED

RUBBLE WAS ALL that remained of this man's home near the Kebo Valley Club after flames swept across his neighborhood on the outskirts of town. In all, 17,188 acres—mostly in Bar Harbor and Acadia National Park—were blackened, 170 houses leveled, and 67 summer cottages destroyed in the Great Fire of 1947.

EPILOGUE

Smoke still wafted from the rubble when the Great Fire of 1947 was finally declared out on Nov. 14, 1947, nearly a month after it started. The hills surrounding Bar Harbor lay scorched, the charred trunks of once-majestic trees protruding like blackened thorns above plains of ash and granite boulders bleached white by the heat.

In many ways, the fire marked the end of Bar Harbor's great cottage era. In truth, however, many of the grand summer homes had previously fallen into disrepair, victims of the Great Depression, the imposition of a federal income tax, and lives put on hold by World War II. Bar Harbor, like Newport, and the grand hotels of the Adirondacks and the Whites, no longer appealed to the next generation of rich and privileged.

With so much of the landscape that once drew tens of thousands of summer swells gone, the community began a conversation about what would come next. It didn't take long before the crowds of visitors, who began arriving in the spring to see the fire's devastation firsthand, provided a clue. Tourism would become the next big thing.

In many ways, Bar Harbor today, at the turn of the 21st century, mirrors that of the 20th. The town is once again home to scores of large hotels. Accommodations from luxury resorts to mom and pop B&Bs, and dozens of weekly vacation rentals provide more than 4,000 rooms and campsites to the more than two million annual visitors. Instead of arriving by coastal steamboat, tens of thousands drop in, for a day at a time, aboard ocean-going cruise ships.

Multi-million dollar summer homes still line the shore. The summer high society social scene remains a whirl, and the yachts of the rich and famous still regularly drop anchor offshore.

Birdseye View from Scotts Hill
Bar Harbor, N

On the hills overlooking the town the verdant forests have returned.
And for those for whom reminders of the magic combination of sea and
shore, of mountains and sky, of bustling villages and quiet retreats, tugs
at the heart, Bar Harbor, Mount Desert Island, and Acadia National
Park will always remain; *Forever Yours.*